Let GOD DRIVE Your BMW

Dr. Verrick Norwood

clfpublishing.org
909.315.3161

Cover design by Senir Design. Contact info: info@senirdesign.com

ISBN #978-1-945102-88-2

Printed in the United States of America.

Dedication

This work is dedicated to the memory of my spiritual father, Prophet Roger Decuir.

One of the last things you prophesied to me before you transitioned to Glory was, "I see another book, son," which was my confirmation. You will never be forgotten. I love you Prophet/Dad, and I close in your famous words, "I believe God."

Acknowledgments

I am truly thankful to God for His love, patience, leading, and guidance.

I am also sincerely thankful for my wife, Mecheco, to whom I will always owe an extremely high debt of appreciation. Through the writer's block, frustrations, praying for and fasting with me, and a list of other things about this book, you were there. You are the epitome of a true best friend and are always there for me (capital A in always). Thanks, babe.

Foreword
by Prophet Dray Scott

I encourage you to buckle up and enjoy the ride that this anointed book is about to take you on. From the very introduction, you are challenged to weigh in the balance of your own mind concepts, such as coincidence or purposeful design, reason or faith, belief and obedience or disbelief and disobedience. *Let God Drive Your BMW* is an open invitation for you to take your relationship to a greater depth of obedience, trust, and reliance on the sovereignty of Him who paid a dear price through the demonstrative exhibit of love and grace.

Foreword
by Dr. C. White-Elliott

Let God Drive Your BMW is an eye opener for those who are looking for spiritual direction in their personal lives. In this earth realm in which we reside, we have been taught and trained to direct our own lives and make our own decisions. In short, we have been taught time and time again to lean to our own understanding, exercising our free will. However, Proverbs 3:5-6 tells us unequivocally to refrain from leaning to our own understanding, but instead to acknowledge God, allowing Him to direct our path.

Let God Drive Your BMW will liberate your thinking as Dr. Verrick Norwood rightly divides the Word of Truth. In the three chapters within, he shares biblical principles and a concrete method for yielding to the Holy Spirit's Will by laying down your own will and receiving all God has in store for you as you follow His leading.

Read, take notes in the margins, highlight, and become liberated in God as you relinquish the keys of your life to the Almighty. Watch your life be changed for the better!

Table of Contents

Introduction

On August 28, 1998, my life took a turn, and at that time, it felt as though things would never get better. I did not realize that what had just happened would be one of the best things that could have ever happened to me. At the time, I was not saved. Therefore, I didn't know Romans 8:28, which reads, *"And we know that all things work together for good to them that love God, to them who are the called according to His purpose."*

My girlfriend at that time, who is now my wife, Mecheco and I had both received a transfer from the company we worked for to relocate to Chicago. Chicago is my hometown, and I had so desired to move back home. At that time, I was residing in Granite City, IL, and Mecheco was residing in Centreville, IL. Mecheco and I were both assistant managers at the company, but we worked at two different locations.

On September 6, 1998, our transfers were scheduled to be in effect. Mecheco and I made plans to take off work on August 26 and 27 to drive to Chicago and find a place to live, so when the transfer was active, we would already be moved in and ready for work. While at work on August 25, 1998, I dropped $36,000 in the company safe, locked up, turned the store alarm on, and went home.

The next morning, on August 26, 1998, I woke up early to drive to Chicago with Mecheco and our daughter Verricka (who is now with the Lord). Our mission was to find a place to live. While we were heading to Chicago, my phone rang. The bookkeeper from the job was calling. She stated that my $36,000 drop was short $1,100. I responded, "Well, I dropped $36,000 like I wrote on the slip, so I don't know how $1,100 is missing." She responded, "Well, you are scheduled to be back at work on the 28th correct?" I said, "Yes." She said, "We will see you then. Be safe."

On August 28, when I returned to work, they fired me stating that because I was the manager on shift the night of the 25th, I was being held responsible for the missing money. "Here is your last check, and you can forget about that transfer because you no longer work for this company," were their final words to me.

Beloved, I was hurt and confused, to say the least. We were looking forward to relocating to my hometown Chicago as a family, but that desire ended on that day. I moved to my hometown Chicago without Mecheco and Verricka. However, before I left for Chicago, I spoke with my mother and asked her if I found a lawyer could she pay whatever his cost was because I wanted to sue the company for wrongful discharge. She agreed to pay the lawyer, and I promised her after I won, I would pay her back.

Well, things didn't work out for me when I moved back to Chicago. I was happy to be home, but I was lonely without Mecheco and Verricka. I eventually moved back to Centreville, IL in 1999 and lived with Mecheco at her parents' house until we found a place to rent. One day, my mom called me and said, "Son, go and find yourself a place and see if they will accept a co-signer from out of town. I will send you the first month and last month's rent." Mecheco and I found a place in O'Fallon, IL and moved in.

When we moved in, I immediately started looking for employment. I went to the gas station, bought a newspaper, and went home. Out of nowhere, I had the thought that I needed to ask God to help me find a job. I had never done that before. At the time, I still was not saved because I didn't know what that was anyway, but I always knew God existed. I had been to church many times while growing up, but I lived how I wanted to live.

When I went into our bedroom, I was home alone. I fell to my knees and said, "God, when I open this paper to the job section, can you please make my eyes fall on the job you want me to have, so I can help some people for you?" Beloved, I went to the job section and closed my eyes. As soon as I opened my eyes, they fell on a job, and it read, "God Will." I wiped my eyes and asked, "What kind of job is this?" So, I looked again, and it read, 'Goodwill Industries for a Community Employment Specialist.'

Beloved, God made my eyes to first see the words 'God Will.' It was as though He answered my prayer to Him when I asked Him, "Can you please make my eyes fall on the job you want me to have, so I can help some people for you?" I immediately sent Goodwill a resume, and they called me the very next day for the job opening for a Community Employment Specialist to schedule me for an interview. I went to the interview the following week in St. Louis, MO, and they hired me on the spot.

Now, beloved, I was still working on my wrongful discharge case. Over a year had passed, and my lawyer was still pressing forward. On the very first day at my new job, I found out that my lawyer's office was right around the corner from my job. Was that a coincidence or divine providence? As

I look back on that day, knowing what I now know about God, I know it was divine providence.

One day after work, I had to go to the lawyer's office to sign some paperwork. When I arrived, his secretary opened the door and said, "Your lawyer is on the phone. When he gets off, he will open his office door and that will be an indication for you to go in to sign." She then showed me where I could sit and wait. While I was waiting, she said, "Veric, I finally have a chance to ask you what I have been waiting to ask because every time you come by, you are in and out." She went on to ask me, "Do you go to church?" I said, "Well, I used to go here and there with my mom while growing up, but as I got older, I am everywhere but church."

She then said, "Veric, I would like to invite you to my church, and if you have three questions that you would love to get answers to if you ask God this week and come on Saturday evening, you will find out that God heard all your questions." I said to myself, *Saturday? Please! That's my drinking day. I will not be at no church.* She gave me the address and repeated, "If you have three questions you would love God to answer if you ask Him this week, you will find out that He heard you if you come Saturday." After she finished handing me the address to the church, my lawyer's door swung open for me to sign my papers.

The next day was Tuesday. I bent over to put my shoes on for work, and while I was putting my shoes on, it was like someone hit a rewind button on the radio and replayed the whole conversation that I had on Monday with my lawyer's secretary. I heard her say *If you just have three questions you would love God to answer.*

The next day, on Wednesday, the same thing happened while I was putting on my shoes. On Thursday, the same thing happened again while I was putting on my shoes. That time I thought, *What would hurt if I go to church on Saturday? I do have three questions I would love God to answer.* I stood up, and I asked Mecheco if she would go to church with me on Saturday evening, and she said yes. I didn't tell her the whole conversation my lawyer's secretary and I had because I didn't want her to know about the three questions because one of them was about her.

On my way to work that Thursday, I said, "Lord, I have three questions for you, and I was told that if I ask, I will get my answers on Saturday if I attend that service. Well, my first question is, 'Am I supposed to marry my baby's mother?' My second question is, 'Why did you put me on this earth? What was I born to do?' My third question is, 'Lord, am I going to win my lawsuit, or am I wasting my time?'"

Beloved, Saturday evening came, and we headed to that service and ended up at a house. When we walked in, it was set up like a church. That was new to me because I never attended a service at a house, not knowing that's how many services were held in biblical times. When we walked in, the lawyer's secretary ran up to us immediately, and I thought, *Please don't ask me if I asked God those questions because I don't want Mecheco to ask me what questions she is talking about.* Because again one of the questions was about her!

The secretary walked us up to the front where the visitors sat, and the church eventually started. They gathered around for worship, and in my mind, I said, *This is nice, though normally I would have a drink in my hand at this time.* After worship, we all sat down, and the pastor went up to his podium and opened his Bible. Then, he paused and looked at me. When he looked at me, he said, "Sir, in the black shirt, stand, please!" He then said, "I am hearing three questions you asked God this week." I thought to myself, *If he gets one right, I'll be convinced that God is amazing.* He went on to say, "One of your questions is about her." Then, he pointed to Mecheco, and she looked at me with a look that asked, "What is he talking about?"

The pastor went on to say, "I hear God saying you asked Him if you are supposed to marry your baby's mother?" I immediately started crying, and that almost made me faint. He said, "God said, 'Yes.' He created her for you and you for her. You two will have a happy marriage." He then said, "I am hearing the second question you asked, and this is a good one. Church, you guys need to ask God this." Looking directly at me, he said, "You asked God: 'Lord, why did you put me on this earth? What was I born to do?'" He said, "God said, 'In your mother's womb, He chose you. You will pastor one day and one day travel this world preaching the Gospel." He then said, "I hear the third question, but God is not giving me the answer only the question, so you will know that He heard you. I hear you asking, 'Lord, am I going to win this lawsuit, or am I wasting my time?'" He added, "Is that what you asked God?" I said, "Yes, word for word."

Beloved, that day was life changing, because I learned that I was to marry my daughter's mother and why God had put me on this earth. The final question was designed for me to find out as time went by. The last words that came out of the pastor's mouth were, "Here, take my number because God said you will need to call me real soon about something."

Two weeks later, I was driving to work, and all of a sudden, I was stuck in traffic. As I sat in traffic, my mind went back to my childhood to a time when my mom had my brothers and me sitting around her bed. She said, "Boys, always remember you can ask God anything." Immediately from that thought, I said, "Lord, my mom told me a long time ago that I can ask you anything. Can you tell me where I am supposed to be because I don't want to live a mediocre life? Can you show me a vision of where you want me to go or something? I don't know much about faith, but I will learn as I go. God, when I close my eyes, can you show me something?" I closed my eyes, and immediately, I saw myself sitting on top of the Hollywood sign, on the "wood" in Hollywood.

The amazing thing is in my last name, the last four letters are the word "wood." When I opened my eyes, I asked, "God, is that you showing me this or is this my imagination? I'm sure many people say you showed them things, but it was their imagination. Lord, if that was you and not my imagination, can you show me one more time?" Beloved, I closed my eyes, and *boom* I was sitting on the word "wood" on the Hollywood sign. I then opened my eyes to the sound of horns blowing at me because I was then holding up traffic.

When I finally arrived at work, I went into my office, and I was reminded of the last words the pastor said to me at that service, to take his number because God said I would need to call him about something. I pulled his number out of my wallet and called the minister. He answered, and I shared the vision. He said, "Well, if it's from God, then there is a meaning to it." So, he prayed and said, "The Lord said you have an imagination of acting, but you will not be an actor. You will be a minister like He told you. The reason why you were sitting on top of the Hollywood sign is that He will take you higher than what Hollywood can take you. Real soon, you will move to California." He continued, "The Lord said, 'All I ask of you is this one thing: Let me go before you, and I will order your steps for as long as you live.'" In my mind, I said, *California!!*

After work, I rushed home and told Mecheco. She said, "You're nuts! First, you ask God questions about me. Now, you're seeing visions about California!" That night, I asked God to show her something. A few weeks later, we revisited that conversation about California. She was then convinced, after God showed her that it was Him speaking to me and showing me signs. She said, "I believe it's God, but how are we going to move to California with no money?" My response was, "I thought the same thing." That morning while I was getting ready for work, I turned the TV on, and a preacher pointed to the camera and said, "If God showed you a vision, He will send the provision." I then fell to my knees and lifted my hands and said, "Lord, you showed me a vision; now, can you send me the provision?" I then said, "Mech, we are moving in August." (It was April 2000 at the time.)

I went on to say, "Let's get married. We have been living like married people for too long, and we have already been told that we were made for one another, so let's go to the courthouse- you, Verricka, and me. I know you want a big wedding, but we can still do that one day. I don't want to go to California with different last names, so let's go to the courthouse first." As soon as we came to an agreement and made preparations for getting married at the courthouse, my lawyer called me and said, "Veric, the company is ready to settle on May 19, 2000. Write down this address, and meet me in the lobby at 9 am."

Beloved, I walked out of the court with a check in my hand for $36,000. God made them give me what I gave them back on August 25, 1998. If you remember, the third question I had asked God before I went to that church was, "Lord, am I going to win my lawsuit, or am I wasting my time?" Well, when I went to that church, the minister repeated my question as God gave it to him, but God didn't answer because I had to wait to find out on May 19, 2000. That was our provision for God's vision to move to California.

Beloved, as I look back on those days, I realize God is a God of purpose. Everything He does/allows is for His purpose for your good. For He desires to reveal to you and me His purpose for our lives. The most important question out of the three questions I asked God was the second one, which was, "Why did you put me on this earth? What was I born to do?" Beloved, what I was asking Him was, "Lord, what is my purpose on this earth?" I have found out in His purpose for our lives is His provision, His protection, His peace, and His everything that we need is wrapped up in His purpose for you and me. Believers all over the world constantly ask this question: How can I find out/know His purpose for my life, as if it's some mystery or a secret/riddle.

My focus in this book is to point you in the right direction from the Word of God on how you can find God's purpose for your life. The Word of God has everything we will ever need.

Recently, my wife and I purchased a car, and the salesman showed us a few things that our car can do and then told us to be sure to look into the manual, so we can find out the other features. Well, if we decide not to open the manual, then the only things we will know is what the salesman showed us.

I found out this is the problem in the Body of Christ; we never open the manual for our life called the Bible/Word of God. We only know what we hear on Sundays and at Bible Study (if we attend) simply because we refuse to open the Bible ourselves to see what else God has for our lives. Today, I want to direct you to the manual for your life: the Bible, so you can see how you can find the God-given purpose for your life. Amazingly, the car we recently purchased is a BMW, and ironically, the title of this book is *Let God Drive Your BMW*!! In so doing, you will know and live out the God-given purpose for your life.

Chapter One
First Key "B"

Beloved, let God drive your BMW!

We find in Luke 9:23-27 some profound words, and I like how it is written in the Message Bible. Notice what Jesus announced then and now: *"Then He told them what they could expect for themselves: Anyone who intends to come with Me has to let Me lead. You're not in the driver's seat - I am. Don't run from suffering: embrace it. Follow Me and I'll show you how. Self-help is no help at all. Self-sacrifice is the way, My way, to finding yourself, your true self. What good would it do to get everything you want and lose you, the real you? If any of you is embarrassed with Me and the way I'm leading you, know that the Son of Man will be far more embarrassed with you when He arrives in all His splendor in company with the Father and the holy angels. This isn't, you realize, pie in the sky by and by. Some who have taken their stand right here are going to see it happen, see with their own eyes the Kingdom of God"* (Luke 9:23-27).

In that passage, Jesus said it comes down to a self-sacrifice. Now, let us move into what a self-sacrifice is, so you can release the keys to your BMW, so Jesus can take the wheel and show you His Will for your life.

In Romans 12:1-2, we find the breakdown of BMW. Jesus said self-sacrifice is the way, which is also His Way. In Paul's writings, we will find at the close of his letters something to apply to our lives. Paul understood that too many believers in the Church are just hearers of the Word. Being just hearers gets us nowhere, but when you apply to your life what you hear, then and only then will you see change. In the Word of God, you will find that hearing and doing will always go together, especially in Paul's writings. Why? Because, our hearing of the Word must become our living.

In Romans 12, Paul speaks about relationships because Paul understood if we desire good and lasting relationships in this life, we must first have the right relationship with the Lord. I John 4:20 announces, *"If a man says, I love God, and hateth his brother, he is a liar! For he that loveth not his brother whom he hath seen, how can he love God whom he hath not seen?"*

In Romans 12 Verse 2, Paul mentions the word "prove." This word comes from the Greek word "dokimazo," which means to test, to prove with expectations of approval. This word was applied to metals, to the operation of testing and trying them to see if the metals are real or not. Beloved, this sounds like relationships because truly relationships will be tested.

To further understand the meaning of the word "prove," I cannot help but think about Psalm 34:8, where it reads, "taste and see that the Lord is good." Tasting is trying/testing, and trying/testing is experiencing. In so doing, you will see the goodness and the realness of the Lord. For Paul to use the word "prove," he was alluding to an intimate relationship because you not only obtain knowledge but also obtain experience. The Bible declares Adam "knew" Eve (Genesis 4:1). The word "knew" means he knew her intimately. Adam did not know her from his head knowledge. No, he knew her from his heart and that came by way of intimacy. Paul is telling us children of God that we can know God's Will for our life intimately by releasing to the Lord three keys from your life into His Hands.

The first key provided in Romans 12:1-2 is called "Body." Paul just finished teaching and drawing our attention to the mercies of God in the previous chapters and is now ready to give his audience a practical application like he always does at the close of his lessons. His practical lesson here comes down to living a holy and dedicated life unto God. Notice this two-letter word in Verse 1: "By." This word points us to the reason why Paul intimates that we do this. He says we should do this because "the mercies of God" have been with us all our life before we came to Christ and since we gave our life to Christ. The word "mercies" here speaks about the favor God has shown us is undeserving, that undeserving compassion and kindness that flows from His heart.

Romans 5:5 says, *"Because the love of God is shed abroad in our hearts by the Holy Ghost which is given unto us."*

Romans 8:1 shows us God's favor that is extended to those who deserve condemnation and even hell but His mercy blocked it all and united us to Him.

Romans 8:9 and 26 inform us that the indwelling Holy Spirit is within believers to guide us, empower us, illuminate us, and even intercede for us simply because of His grace and mercy. These are just a few verses of God's mercy on display.

The mercies of God spared us all from that which we deserved: HELL. One cannot help but appreciate and embrace the mercies of God once experienced in salvation when you understand and are conscious of the fact that we have not received what we truly deserved. It is this kind of mercy Paul is speaking about to his audience, alluding to the fact that this is the reason we should live a holy and dedicated life unto God.

Holy/Holiness does not mean perfect and/or never making mistakes. The Bible admonishes us to, *"Follow peace with all men, and holiness"* (Hebrews 12:14). Holiness comes from the Greek word "hagios." This gives us the meaning of one that is separate and/or different. Not one that dresses differently but lives a godly lifestyle. The writer here in Hebrews is alluding to his audience that you are not to live like the world, act like the world, and think like the world because how you think is how you will walk/live. God has called His children to a higher level- period. The Holy Spirit has been sent to the believer to help us live holy unto God. There is no excuse that we cannot live the way God desires because He sent us His Spirit to help. The word "follow" in Hebrews 12:14 means to pursue, seek, and hunt after. It alludes to the fact that we should be like a hunter seeking after an animal to catch. We are to seek, pursue, and hunt after a holiness lifestyle unto God. This kind of lifestyle is a different and separate kind of lifestyle.

In Rankin Wilbourne's book, *Union with Christ*, he asserts holiness to be, "The Big Broccoli in the Sky." He says, "Holiness is like broccoli for many of us. We know we are supposed to want it, but we don't, not really. And we might even think the good news is that we no longer need to pursue it." Wilbourne speaks on the prevailing neglect of holiness among the people of God. He asserts, "God wants us to grow in holiness, not as some sort of test or punishment, not even just as preparation for the future, but because he wants us to enjoy life with Him more. The more we grow in holiness, the more we can enjoy His presence. He wants us not simply to press on but to soar." Furthermore, Brother J. I. Packer, the author of *Rediscovering Holiness: Know the Fullness of Life with God,* retorted, "In reality, holiness is the goal of redemption. As Christ died in order that we may be sanctified, so we are justified in order that we may be sanctified and made holy." Here now, we find that holiness comes from a position in a place called total surrender unto God, which paints a picture of a life that is well pleasing to God and Him alone.

As I look back over my life, I can never forget how I used my "body" for sinful gratification and intentions. Right about now someone is probably saying, "Me as well." Beloved, now that we understand and recognize Whose we are, it is time we use our "bodies" for Him, our Lord and Savior. Paul informs his audience in I Cor. 6:19-20 that the believer's body is God's temple. Notice these words, *"What? Know ye not that your body is the temple of the Holy Ghost which is in you, which ye have from God, and ye are not your own? For ye are bought with a price: therefore glorify God in your body, and in your spirit, which are God's."* Yes, because the believer's body is where the Holy Spirit dwells. *"But ye are not in the flesh, but in the Spirit, if so be that the Spirit of God dwell in you"* (Romans 8:9).

Luke 12:48 declares, *"To whom much is given, much will be required."* The Holy Spirit has been given to the believer to help us live for God here on earth, and there is no better

Gift. Therefore, we are required to live holy. It is an honor and a benefit to live for/with Christ and magnify Him in this body. Paul said, *"According to my earnest expectation and my hope, that in nothing I shall be ashamed, but that with all boldness, as always, so now also Christ shall be magnified in my body, whether it be life, or death. For to me to live is Christ, and to die is gain"* (Philippians 1:20-21).

When Jesus was born in Bethlehem, we understand He stepped into a human body, so He could fulfill the Will of the Father. He didn't put on a costume or outfit that looked like a body. No, He was in a real body. He yielded Himself and became a true servant in a real body. This is what we as His followers must do: yield our bodies to Him and Him alone, so Jesus can continue His purpose through us here on earth. Paul tells us how we are to yield, Beloved, in Romans 6:12-13, which says, *"Let not sin therefore reign in your mortal body, that ye should obey it in the lusts thereof, neither yield ye your members as instruments of unrighteousness unto sin: but yield yourselves unto God."*

Beloved, God desires to use our bodies as His tools for building His Kingdom of light and as His weapons to fight the kingdom of darkness. When we yield to Him, we become pliable in His Hands like a tool in a carpenter's hand and an instrument in a musician's hand.

When Paul stood before his audience and delivered this clarion announcement for Jesus' followers to present their bodies to Him "as a living sacrifice," we find he went back into the Old Testament vernacular in books like Leviticus and Numbers, where they used words like sacrificial offerings. Bless God, for He has done away with the old system and Jesus came to establish a new one. The same term "sacrifice" is used, but it is not done the same way. Hebrews 8:13 asserts, *"In speaking of the new covenant, He hath made the first old. Now that which decayeth and waxeth old is ready to vanish away."*

Believers today have become one body in Christ beginning with Jews and Gentiles (Gal. 3:27-29). Therefore, those of us who are followers of Christ share in this God-given new covenant that was procured on the Cross. These blessings of the new covenant are practiced and adapted to individuals.

In Romans 12, we find a New Testament sacrificial order and/or method. R. C. Sproul's shares his thoughts, which I believe are conducive with the New Testament standards. He tells us it is not a sacrifice we give because atonement has been made for us. God does not ask us to bring in our livestock and burn them on the altar. Rather, He asks us to give ourselves, to put ourselves alive on the altar. To be a Christian means to live a life of sacrifice, a life of presentation, making a gift of ourselves to God.

We are blessed to have two examples of "living sacrifices" in the Word of God to help us understand and ascertain that which Paul is announcing here Romans 12:1. Our first example is located in the Old Testament, and this individual went by the name Isaac. One day, God awakened Abraham, Isaac's father, and said, *"Take now thy son, thine only son Isaac, whom thou lovest, and get thee into the land of Moriah: and offer him there for a burnt offering upon one of the mountains which I will tell thee of"* (Genesis 22:2).

It is amazing to me how Isaac and our Savior Jesus are so similar. For instance, Isaac was conceived by way of a miracle. His parents Abraham and Sarah were senior citizens, and Sarah was born barren- but God. Jesus was born of a virgin, which means He came by way of a miracle. Isaac was a promise spoken by God to his parents many, many years before he arrived. Jesus' birth was promised way back in Genesis 3:15, and only God knows how many years ago that was spoken.

Isaac's parents, Abraham and Sarah, were told by God to name him Isaac. Jesus' earthly parents, Mary and Joseph, were also told by God what to name Him. Isaac, via his father Abraham, willingly put himself on the altar and would have died in obedience to God's Will, but thanks be to God, He had other plans. *"And Abraham lifted up his eyes, and looked, and behold behind him a ram, and offered him up for a burnt offering in the stead of his son"* (Gen 22:13).

God sent a ram to take Isaac's place. However, Isaac died spiritually just like the ram died in the natural. Isaac died to self and was quick to yield in all willingness unto the will of God. When Isaac climbed off the altar, he became our first example of a living sacrifice "holy, acceptable unto God" (Romans 12:1).

What I find amazing is the mindset of our heavenly Father. Notice Genesis 22:2c: *"and get thee into the land of Moriah."* This is God telling Abraham to take his son to make a sacrifice at this certain place. Now "Moriah" literally means "foreseen of Jehovah." It is as though God is saying, "Look, Abraham. This is what I want you to do for me. I want you to take your son to Moriah, and when you get there, you will give the world a vision, a preview, and a peek of that which is to come. Yes, because I will sacrifice my only Begotten Son at this same place which I have called you to Abraham."

Beloved, Moriah (according to what I have studied) is a ridge that runs from north to south through the city of

Jerusalem, right outside of the north wall of the city at a place called Calvary. God told Abraham also in Genesis 22:2, *"and offer him there for a burnt offering."* The word "offer" means "to lift up." It alludes to the fact that Abraham lifted Isaac up upon Mt. Moriah unto God. I am reminded of the book of John where Jesus said, *"And I, if I be lifted up from earth, will draw all men unto Me"* (12:32). Beloved, why did He say this? I'm glad you ask because we find the answer in the very next verse. *"He said this to indicate how He was going to die"* (John 12:33).

Jesus, just like Isaac, was obedient unto His Father even unto death. This leads me to our second example of a "living sacrifice." Jesus Christ is truly our ultimate and perfect model simply because He died as a sacrifice. But thanks be to God, Jesus rose in three days. Today, right now, and forever Jesus is in heaven as a perfect "living sacrifice" with the scars and bruises to prove He went to Calvary to die on the cross and rose in three days.

"Seeing then that we have a great High Priest, that is passed into the heavens, Jesus the Son of God, let us hold fast our profession. For we have not a High Priest which cannot be touched with the feeling of our infirmities; but was in all points tempted like as we are, yet without sin. Let us, therefore, come boldly unto the throne of grace, that we may obtain mercy, and find grace to help in time of need" (Hebrews 4:14-16).

Jesus is our High Priest with His Arms always open for His children to come to Him, not timid or laisser-faire, but boldly. Jesus has the grace and the mercy we need to keep us in His race because the price has been paid, and the work was finished on Calvary. His mercy and grace are two reasons why we should *"present your body a living sacrifice, holy, acceptable unto God, which is your reasonable service"* (Romans 12:1).

We find here in Verse 1 these words "reasonable service" (in the King James version). However, we also find these words "spiritual worship" in the Revised Standard Version, which has the same meaning; it is just worded differently. What is Paul saying to us who believe? What should we gather from these terms for our day-by-day walk with God? The words "reasonable service" and/or "spiritual worship" are two words used in the Greek text "logikos" and "latreia." It is interesting that "logikos" is where our English word "logical" is derived from, and it can mean either "rational, genuine, and true" or in a figurative sense, "spiritual."

"Latreia" can be translated as "worship" or "service" and is used in describing religious service to God. So, whether we translate this profound phrase "reasonable service" or "spiritual worship" or any other version, people will grasp this mindset that our spiritual worship is our logical and reasonable service, considering God's mercies that are extended to all of us.

John Stott, author of *The Message of Romans: God's Good News for the World*, brings a nice application I believe is worthy to be mentioned. He retorts, "What is the living sacrifice, this rational, spiritual worship? It is not to be offered in the temple courts or in the church building, but rather in home life and in the marketplace. It is the presentation of our bodies to God." I like this mindset because the Body of Christ often thinks of worship as something we just do at church, but true worship is a lifestyle that involves every part of you.

When we present our life to God in this way, then and only then does our worship become a reasonable, logical response.

Through His death, reconciliation with God has come to a fallen people. Those who trust in Him are restored to offer true worship in spirit and truth (John 4:23-24). This is truly a slight and partial experience of that great and awesome worship gathering of all God's children whom He has redeemed who will worship Him forever in the New Creation (Rev. 7:9-12). Understanding we have been redeemed brings transformation to our hearts and births in us a new heart that hungers and thirsts to worship Him and Him only. It was David who declared, *"Let the redeemed of the Lord say so, whom He has redeemed from the hand of the enemy"* (Psalm 107:2).

Beloved, our daily worship unto God truly makes sense in the light of His awesome grace and mercy He has bestowed on our lives. God is most definitely worthy of this kind of offering, and knowing this, we must see this as a privilege and honor to present our body unto Him as a living sacrifice.

It's amazing to me how Abraham understood when God told him to *"Take now your son, your only son Isaac, whom you love, and go to the land of Moriah, and offer him there as a burnt offering on one of the mountains of which I shall tell you"* (Gen. 22:2). Abraham perceived this as worship. Notice what he said to his men, *"And Abraham said to his young men, stay here with the donkey; the lad and I will go yonder and worship, and we will come back to you"* (Gen. 22:5). These words came from a heart full of faith that was derived from an intimate love relationship. Only this kind of relationship can speak with that kind of assurance.

I am reminded of a woman by the name of Mary in the Bible. Worship is seen very profoundly in her life. I believe her example is apropos right about now. Every time you see this particular Mary in the Bible, she is worshipping at the feet of Jesus. Notice these two verses, *"Then took Mary a pound of ointment of spikenard, very costly, and anointed the feet of Jesus, and wiped His feet with her hair: and the house was filled with the odour of the ointment"* (John 12:3). Matthew tells us, *"There came unto Him a woman having an alabaster box of very precious ointment, and poured it on His head, as He sat at meat"* (26:7).

Now, Matthew tells us she had an "alabaster box," which means before she was able to pour the ointment upon Jesus, she first had to break the box open. Here, we find something profound about worship. Worship that is real and authentic and oftentimes comes from that broken place in one's life. Because when we are truly broken, we become meek and humble unto the Lord.

I don't know about you, Beloved, but I know about that broken place because I have truly experienced brokenness in my life before Christ and since I have been walking with Christ. Another thing we see about worship in Mary's life is also profound. John said the ointment was "very costly." True worship, Beloved, will cost us something. Paul said, *"present your bodies a living sacrifice"* (Romans 12:1). The verb "present" here means to present once and for all. It is a command that is a well-defined commitment of the body to the Lord Almighty. We can liken this to a bride and groom on their wedding ceremony as these two individuals commit themselves to one another. This once and for all commitment impels what they will do with their bodies. This is the kind of body that God must have if He is to express His perfect will through us to the world. He wants our brains, eyes, ears, tongue, hands, and feet as the automobile for His Divine character.

This kind of lifestyle is what it costs for true worship as His followers. Presenting our bodies as "living sacrifices" is the first key to our life that we must give Him. A key called "B for Body." Beloved, what we do with these bodies now will decide our reward or loss on the day called Judgment Day. One thing is for sure: We as believers will stand before God, *"that each one may receive the things done in the body, according to what he has done, whether good or bad"* (2 Corinthians 5:10). It's amazing that we are not going to be judged for this or that sin questions per say that Jesus went to the Cross for, but we will be judged on the service you and I have carried out in this body here on earth. Beloved, until we surrender our key called "B for Body," God can never use us like He desires for His Will/Glory.

Beloved, allow me to pray:

Spirit of the Living God, thank You for this opportunity to pray. It was You, oh God, that gave us the perfect example through Your Son Jesus who actually died and rose in three days and became a "Living Sacrifice." Because of Your Grace and Mercy, you have helped us to present ourselves to You this day as a "Living Sacrifice, holy, and acceptable." Father, I understand we can never earn or deserve forgiveness; therefore, may we all be motivated and encouraged to serve You with gratitude. Continue Precious Holy Spirit to remind us the need to pursue holiness daily. Without it, no man/woman will see You, oh God. Father in the Name of

Jesus, from this day moving forward, help us all to love what You love and hate what You hate. Father. Keep us away from the spirit of pride, fear, and self-righteousness, so the fragrance on our life will bring unto You that which is sweet, full of love, and faith, and be well-pleasing in Your sight and nostrils, in Jesus' matchless name! Amen!!!

Chapter Two
Second Key "M"

Beloved, let God drive your BMW!

Not only are we to give God our "Body," but we must also give God our "Mind." Paul said something interesting in Ephesians 4:17, *"This I say, therefore, and testify in the Lord, that ye henceforth walk not as other Gentiles walk, in the vanity of their mind."*

David prayed one day, *"Create in me a clean heart"* (Psalm 51:10). Why did David pray *"create in me a clean heart"*? Because he knew he could not do it himself. However, Paul reveals to us that we do have the wherewithal to change our minds. Oftentimes, we as believers of Christ justify our actions or habits and never own up to them, but I learned if I change my mind, my God in heaven will change my heart. Food for thought, Beloved: God will not change our hearts until we first change our minds.

There is a reason why Paul said, *"Let this mind be in you which was also in Christ Jesus"* (Phil. 2:5). The "mind" of Christ simply means the "attitude" Christ demonstrated. We find in the NIV version these words, *"your attitude should be the same as that of Christ"* (Phil. 2:5). On this walk with Christ, we will find our outlook always determines our outcome. *"For as he thinketh in his heart, so is he"* (Prov. 23:7). If your outlook is all about me, myself, and I, your outcome will not be good in the end. How we think is how we act, live, walk, and talk.

The second key provided in Romans 12:1-2 is "M for Mind." *"And be not conformed to this world: but be ye transformed by the renewing of your mind"* (Romans 12:2a). This cruel world endeavors to control our minds, Beloved. But, God our Father in heaven endeavors to transform our minds.

Apostle Paul understood both sides of the streets: a conformed street and a transformed street. One day, Paul was on the road heading to Damascus. At that time, his name was still Saul, who was an angry man out of control. Notice these words, *"And as he journeyed, he came near Damascus: and suddenly there shined round about him light from heaven: and he fell to the earth, and heard a voice saying unto him, Saul, Saul, why persecutest thou Me?"* (Acts 9:3-4).

It is amazing how life can all of a sudden take a turn. You thought you were going in one direction, but life took a sudden turn. Saul was on his way to murder some believers, and God showed up out of the blue. Without warning, life tends to take sudden turns. I often think about December 15, 2017. On that day, my daughter had an accident that took her from this earth. Accidents bring turns in people's lives. Loss of a spouse or child brings a turn in people's life. We find in the hour called grief and heartache, that life and family life are impacted forever. An airplane crashes out of nowhere and brings an unexpected turn in the lives of many families that probably first heard about the crash on the news. Or, the words from your primary doctor, "Sorry to inform you of this news. We got the results from your biopsy, and they don't look good.

Looks like cancer." The individual's life took a turn out of the blue.

In these types of turns in this thing called life, if you are a believer, your spirit will eventually awaken and remind you God is in control. Throughout Paul's life, up to the Damascus Road, he controlled his own life. Then, God took the driver's seat. Paul's conversion/transformation is emphasized in the book of Acts (9:1-9; 22:6-11; 26:12-18).

Paul learned he was called to live a different lifestyle. He understood he was not put on the earth to live in conformity to the world and its system but to be forever transformed into the image of Jesus Christ. That was why he was able to pen these words about Jesus: *"Who gave himself for our sins, that he might deliver us from this present evil world, according to the will of God and our Father"* (Galatians 1:4). Paul realized he could no longer live according to the lifestyle of his past; it had to be put aside. The best thing that happened in Paul's life was when his life took that turn on the road to Damascus. Romans 12:2a gives us hope for a way out of the ways and mindsets of the world.

It is amazing how certain turns in life provoke us to make the ultimate turn. Jesus said one day, *"Repent: for the Kingdom of God is at hand"* (Matthew 4:17). The word "repent" here means "to change one's mind and act on that change." Beloved, just like Paul and many others learned, certain turns in life cause us to turn from how we used to think to how we are supposed to think and live according to that mindset. John 10:10b asserts to us that Jesus came so we would not only have life but to have it more abundantly. Sadly, oftentimes our thoughts hold us back from living the abundant life Jesus came and died for and rose to give us: a victorious and transformed life. This same verse John 10:10a reveals to us, *"the thief cometh not, but for to steal, and to kill, and to destroy."* Yes, he came to steal, kill, and destroy the minds of the believer by any means necessary.

One of the enemy's traps and/or plans is to get us to conform. Paul said here in Romans 12:2a, *"And be not conformed to this world."* Paul is encouraging the believer to resist these pressures that the devil puts around him/her to conform to the world's plots and ways. Paul understood then what we see now in this world system and its terrible values, goals, ideologies, and reasonings that are contrary to God's sovereign will. John reveals to us that this world system is forever passing away. *"And the world passeth away, and the lust thereof"* (1 John 2:17). We find in our Constitution that we are given the right to pursue happiness, which leads many people to live a compromised life to gain the approval of the world. In doing so, we live according to this world system, believing we will be happy.

The world has always and will always bring pressure on the Body of Christ to conform to its standards and changes. This world system refuses to be involved in God's standards. The world sees a so-called good Christian or nice Christian as one who is open and sincere with other religions and world views. This calls for the believer to make accommodations and compromises, so he/she will be able to pull up a seat and sit at the table with the who's who on the world stage.

The believer who has the mindset to be open and sincere is living a life/lie that retorts, "I'm in agreement with whatever you believe is equal to my belief. After all, all roads lead to heaven." This kind of life does not line up with God's Word. Jesus said, *"I am the way, the Truth, and the Life: no man cometh unto the Father, but by Me"* (John 14:6). Jesus is saying I am the absolute only way. Take it or leave it.

If there were many paths to our Father in heaven and many roads to Him for eternal life, my question is, "Why did God sacrifice His Son on Calvary?" Some say, "Well, let's just be more open-minded about heaven." Another question I have is, "Name someone else who died for you and me for our sins?" When you get through thinking, the only name you can come up with is Jesus. When the Apostles were faced with all kinds of persecution, they announced, *"Neither is their salvation in any other: for there is none other name under heaven given among men, whereby we must be saved"* (Acts 4:12).

Jesus made it plain one day when He spoke to Pontius Pilate, who had a worldly mindset just like the world today. Notice these words, *"Then Pilate said to him, Art thou a King then? Jesus answered thou sayest that I am a King. To this end was I born, and for this cause came I into the world, that I should bear witness unto the truth. Every one that is of the truth heareth my voice"* (John 18:37). Worldly Pilate's response was just like the world's today, *"Pilate saith unto Him, what is truth?"* (John 18:38).

Beloved, one thing is for sure in the Body of Christ: You are either a conformer or a transformer. We look at the latest outfits and try to fit in them. We look at the latest cars/homes and go broke trying to pay for them every month. We try to get into the so-called popular group to fit in. When you think about conformers and transformers, you can liken them to a thermometer and thermostat. The problem with many of us in the Body of Christ is that we are one way today and another way tomorrow depending on what we see, hear, and how we feel.

Therefore, we make adjustments in the environment we find ourselves in. These individuals are likened to a conformer/thermometer. Then, we find in the Body of Christ the group that is focused; they know exactly what they are after. Their mind is set and refuses to change. They are connected with those who are focused, and they understand that their temperature on their walk must be either hot or cold but never lukewarm. This group, however, prefers to be hot. This group consists of those who are transformers/thermostat. Question- "Which one are you?"

"And be not conformed to this world, but be ye transformed by the renewing of your mind" (Romans 12:2a). When we look at the word "mind," the key word is between the "m" and the "d." The word "in" tells us where the transformation comes from. Let's look at the word "transformed" now. The word "transform" is the same word we find in Matthew 17:2, which reads, *"And was transfigured before them."* This word here "transfigured" is also "transform." This word has entered into our English language as the word "metamorphosis." This word paints the picture of a change that comes from within.

As I stated earlier, the key word in "mind" is the word "in." This makes sense because this world knows that once your mind is conformed to this world system, you will exert and expend energy from without. However, when the Holy Spirit changes our minds by imparting power from within, your life will be controlled by the word/Holy Spirit. The key to this is the "mind," which is the controlling point of one's thoughts, feelings, and actions.

Beloved, what we put into our mind truly matters. Today, more than I have ever seen in all the years I have been on this earth, we have continual ways to information, arts, entertainment, and just plain foolery. We have to be cognizant when we desire to spend some me time and/or quiet time simply because we will always be invaded with words/ideas that can impact our thoughts.

How do we contend with the wrong thoughts and past experiences that impact the way we think? Sometimes, our answers to certain questions are right in front of our eyes. Notice the letters in "world." If we take the letter "l" out, we find our answer "word." It was Jesus who said, *"Man shall not live by bread alone, but by every word that proceeded out of the mouth of God"* (Matthew 4:4).

I am reminded of what King David retorted in the book of Psalms, *"I am but a foreigner here on earth; I need the guidance of your commands. Don't hide them from me!"* (Psalm 119:19). David viewed God's Word like a map to guide him. He said he is, "a foreigner here on earth." There-fore, he needed some guidance.

I cannot help but think about when we moved to California back in 2000. We went to the gas station, and my eyes fell on a book called the Thomas Guide. I asked the cashier what it was, and he said, "This book will take you to wherever you need to go if you don't know your way around here." Beloved, it is a known fact almost any long trip will require a map or some sort of guide.

As we all travel through this thing called life, the Word of God should be our road map that points us to the safe routes, stumbling blocks to avoid, and onto God's destination for our life. We must see ourselves like David saw himself as a foreigner, traveling here on earth who understands the need to study God's road map, so we may learn His Way.

If we shun His map, we will go in circles through life and run the risk of missing our God-ordained destination. God's Word makes us wise and truly wiser than our adversaries and wiser than anyone who shuns it. Wisdom comes from allowing what God teaches to lead and guide us.

Rick Renner, in his book *Sparkling Gems Volume 1,* speaks about the Word very well. He says, "God's Word brings a supernatural cleansing that washes your mind and emotions from the contamination of the world, the memories of past experiences, and the lies that the enemy has tried to sow into your brain. When you make it a priority to fill your mind with truth from God's Word, the enemy can't penetrate your mind and he can't fill you with his lies. You won't be speaking and confessing untrue things. You see, when your mind is renewed to the Word of God, you become inwardly strengthened and very hard to deceive. Satan knows empty heads are easy to deceive. That's why he loves it when he finds a believer who has made no effort to fill his mind with truth from God's Word."

We must fall in love with the Word of God. It is the Word, the Truth, and the time that we spend with our Lord that makes all the difference. In this intimate time with the Lord, the Holy Spirit pours His thoughts into us, and in so doing, our mind is being renewed daily. John 8:31-32 declares, *"If you continue in my Word, then you are My disciples indeed; and you shall know the truth, and the truth shall make you free."* A disciple is disciplined. He/she continues to pay attention to and make the Word his/her top priority.

Beloved, the more truth we know of the Word the more transformation we will experience. We as followers of Christ must take on a surrendered mindset. I learned a daily transformation must take place in our life. It is that surrendered person who is no longer conformed to this world because his/her life is set apart. He/She who follows Christ should be one who looks differently; there should be a distinctiveness about him/her. God's desire is for His followers to look/act like His Son. Jesus told His disciples one day, *"You did not choose Me, but I chose you, and appointed you that you should go and bear fruit, and that your fruit should remain, that whatever you ask the Father in My name He may give to you"* (John 15:16).

This is the reason why He has chosen/called us to follow. Therefore, we must continue and/or abide in His Word. It is a known fact that what controls your mind controls you. If one desires to live an abundant, blessed, transformed life, it starts by abiding in His Word. God transforms our minds and makes us spiritually minded by using His Word. When the follower of Christ is totally yielded, a changed life is inevitable.

"But we all, with open face beholding as in a glass the glory of the Lord, are changed into the same image from glory to glory, even as by the Spirit of the Lord" (II Corinthians 3:18). We are all changed not because of some program, not some practice, and not some procedure. Beloved, we are changed by the Son of Man named Jesus. *"Looking unto Jesus the author and finisher of our faith; who for the joy that was set before him endured the cross, despising the shame, and is set down at the right hand of the throne of God"* (Hebrews 12:2).

We are changed by looking to Jesus, by spending time with Him, His Word, learning more about Him, imitating Him, and praising/worshipping Him consistently. I'm reminded of a song by Tramaine Hawkins, and some of the words are, "A change, a change has come over me, He changed my life and now I'm free, He washed away all my sins, and made me whole, He washed me white as snow, He changed, my life complete, and now I sit, I sit at His feet, To do what must be done, I'll work and work, until He comes, A wonderful change has come over me."

Turning our minds over to the hands of God is the second key to our life that we must give Him, a key called "M for Mind."

Beloved, allow me to pray:

Spirit of the Living God, thank You for this opportunity to pray once again. Father, I ask You to help us keep our minds submitted, committed, and stayed on You and You alone. You said, *"Thou will keep him in perfect peace, whose mind is stayed on thee: because he trusteth in thee"* (Isaiah 26:3). Let our minds always be in Your Hands and constantly renewed by Your Word. Father, put a wall around us from head to toe, so the enemy has no access to our minds. I ask You to let the Power of Your Word and Precious Holy Spirit flow into every area of our minds, bodies, and souls now and forever, in Jesus' Name!!!

Chapter Three
Third Key "W"

Beloved, let God drive your BMW!

After Paul said, *"And be not conformed to this world: but be ye transformed by the renewing of your mind"* (Romans 12:2a), he then closed with these words, *"that ye may prove what is the good, and acceptable, and perfect will of God"* (Romans 12:2b). Paul went in this order because he understands our mind controls our body, and our will controls our minds. The third key provided in Romans 12:1-2 is "W for Will." One of the blessings of a transformed mind/life is the wisdom, knowledge, and discernment to *"prove what is that good, and acceptable, and perfect will of God"* (Romans 12:2b).

Paul teaches us through experience the downfall of relying on and/or depending on our so-called "will power." Notice what he retorted, *"for that which I do I allow not: for what I would, that do I not; but what I hate, that do I. If then I do that which I would not, I consent unto the law that it is good. Now then it is no more I that do it, but sin that dwelleth in me. For I know that in me (that is in my flesh) dwelleth no good thing: for to will is present with me: but how to perform that which is good I find not. For the good that I would not, that I do. Now if I do that I would not, it is no more I that do it, but sin dwelleth in me. I find then a law, that, when I would do good, evil is present with me"* (Romans 7:15-21).

Paul is speaking of his old nature. He recognizes that though he is saved and filled with the Holy Spirit, the Christian body, mind, and will can still be controlled by the old nature or the new nature, be it flesh or spirit. Paul broke down two problems. First, he desires to do good, but he cannot. Second, he finds himself doing the bad things he does not want to do.

Some may look at these verses and think Paul was a bad guy. No, not at all. Paul is asserting here that of himself, it was impossible for him to obey God's law, and whenever he attempted to do so, evil was knocking at his door. No matter what he did, his doing was contaminated by sin. If you look at those verses, you will find "I" mentioned many times. Paul is alluding to the fact that the problem is not God's law. The problem comes down to "I." Therefore, he found out only when he yielded his will power to God that he was able to see/experience God's power.

Beloved, we find all throughout the Bible that our God is sovereign and powerful. He controls and regulates this universe with a focus and prearranged purpose that everything and everyone will eventually fall to their knees unto Christ our Lord. It was Paul that recorded, *"That at the name of Jesus every knee should bow, of things in heaven, and things in earth, and things under earth: And that every tongue should confess that Jesus Christ is Lord, to the glory of God the Father"* (Philippians 2:10-11). Some of Paul's writings reveal the sovereign will of God. His sovereign will comes down to the redeeming work of Christ, His Son.

Through Christ, He will unite things, *"Then cometh the end, when he shall have delivered up the Kingdom to God, even the Father; when he shall have put down all rule and all authority and power. For he must reign, till he hath put all enemies under his feet. The last enemy that shall be destroyed is death, for he hath put all things under his feet. But when he saith all things are put under him, it is manifest that he is expected, which did put all things under him. And when all things shall be subdued unto him, then the Son also himself be subject unto him that put all things under him, that God may be all in all"* (1 Corinthians 15:24-28).

God has a sovereign will set for this world. Just as sure as His Son Jesus Christ died for this world and rose in three days, He will also return. This is God's sovereign will, *"Behold, he cometh with clouds; and every eye shall see him, and they also which pierced him; and all kindreds of the earth shall wail because of him, even so, Amen"* (Revelation 1:7).

We also find in Paul's writings that God also has a commanded will, and Paul points to it in Romans 12:2, where it reads, *"that ye may prove what is that good, and acceptable, perfect will of God."* I love these words "good and acceptable and perfect." This verse alone should provoke every believer to desire to know God's will for their life. God's will is good, that is, wholesome in its outcome in our lives. So, we need not be afraid or worry about the outcome when obeying Him. Paul said His will is acceptable, which means it is pleasing. It is never annoying or egregious.

John said it best, *"For this is the love of God, that we keep his commandments: and his commandments are not grievous"* (1 John 5:3). Paul goes on to say that His will is perfect, which means mature with no flaws. Romans 12:2b is an invitation to know why God put you and me on this earth. Knowing His will for your life is the best joy on earth you can obtain. One can never be in the center of His will until he/she first yields and submits and be willing to do what it takes to find out His will for his/her life.

Sadly though, for many believers, the idea of knowing the will of God is like a conundrum, mystery, or fantasy. Instead of allowing God's Word and precious Holy Spirit to reveal their steps and path, many live in the dark, being selfish, and leaning on their own understanding. Thanks be to God, Paul points the believer on the right pursuit in Romans 12:2b with these words: "that we may prove" His will for our lives. The word "prove" also reads "discern" in another translation. It comes down to one testing and approving something to be valuable and true. Paul is painting a picture to his audience by using the term "prove" to imply that we as believers should be motivated and determined to pursue and know God's will for our lives.

One of the most prevalently asked questions in the Body of Christ is, "How can I find out God's will for my life?" I believe this is Paul's focus here in Romans 12:2b, because he understood that testing and discerning the will of God is a series of actions that has the tendency to bring together the ways of God through relationships, certain opportunities, aspirations, and situations in life.

Jesus' mindset about pursuing and doing the will of God stands out in His Word. For instance, Jesus retorted, *"Not every one that saith unto me, Lord, Lord, shall enter into the Kingdom of heaven; but he that doeth the will of my Father which is in heaven"* (Matthew 7:21).

There will come a day called "Judgement Day," and the question is how do we prepare for that day? The answer is by doing the will of God. Obedience to His will is what it comes down to. This proves your faith in Him and your love for Him. It is not about confessing "Lord, Lord," and never doing what He says -be it spoken or written.

Too many believers quote the Bible from front to back but never do His will for their lives. When we are born again, we are then filled with His Spirit, *"But ye are not in the flesh, but in the Spirit, if so be that the Spirit of God dwell in you. Now if any man have not the Spirit of God, he is none of His"* (Romans 8:9). We are blessed to know that His Spirit that dwells in the believer enables us to know and do the Father's will. The love of God in our heart provokes us to obey Him. (Well, it should). He gave us this love for Him, *"And hope maketh not ashamed; because the love of God is shed abroad in our hearts by the Holy Ghost which is given unto us"* (Romans 5:5).

The mindset to know and do the will of God fell on Paul so much so he declared these words to the Ephesians, *"Wherefore be ye not unwise, but understanding what the will of the Lord is"* (Ephesians 5:17). Paul said, "be not unwise." In other words, be not foolish in the occupation of your time and in your way of life. Rather, be wise pursuing to understand what God's will is for your life. This word "understanding" here implies to use our minds to ascertain and do the will of God. Paul is alluding to the fact that we ascertain God's will for our lives as God transforms our minds (Romans 12:1-2). God did not give us a mind to put to the side; no, He gave us a mind for us to give it back to Him, so He can transform it, so we can know His will and do it.

Paul said something interesting in Ephesians 2:10: *"for we are his workmanship, created in Christ Jesus unto good works, which God hath before ordained that we should walk in them."* Notice the word "workmanship." This comes from the Greek word "poiema." Rick Renner breaks this word down as follows, "The word poiema carries the idea of something that is artfully created. The Greek word for poet, *poietes*, comes from this same word. In reference to a poet, this Greek word would denote one who has the extraordinary ability to write or create a literary masterpiece. Paul uses the word 'poiema' to explain what happened when you became a child of God. It emphatically means that on the day you got saved, God put forth His most powerful and creative effort to make you anew. Once God finished making you anew, you became a masterpiece, skillfully, and artfully created in Christ Jesus. There's nothing cheap about you at all! God's creative, artistic, intelligent genius went into your making."

The word "workmanship" all by itself informs us that God has an ordained plan for you and me. Therefore, we should seek Him daily, so we may discover and ascertain His will and do it. Then and only then can we walk attentively and meticulously because we will know what God's will is for our life. I am reminded of my twin brother who works on houses and sells them when he is done. He starts with a blueprint and uses it as his guide to accomplish what was planned from the beginning. God's will for our lives is our blueprint, and the Holy Spirit is our guide. If we follow Him closely, He will help us accomplish what God planned from the beginning.

Beloved, one of the things I love about Jesus is He will never require something from us He has not done first. He was not the kind of teacher who said do as I say but rather do as I do.

Amazingly, we find that Jesus wrestled with the temptation to disobey His Father's will; therefore, He understands how that happens to all of us. When it was coming to that hour for Him to go to the Cross and do the Father's will, the thought troubled Him and gripped Him ferociously. His blood dripped like sweat through the pores of His skin. While He humbled Himself in the darkness in the Garden of Gethsemane, He staggered and was falling so much so His thoughts kept returning to challenge His determination. I'm sure He thought, *Why must I suffer for these people?* knowing He would still be holy and righteous if He allowed the world to suffer the consequences of our disobedience.

Uncommonly, nothing drove Him to fulfill His mission, except His love for the world and His obedience to His Father. He said, *"O my Father, if it is possible, let this cup pass from Me, nevertheless not as I will, but as thou wilt"* (Matthew 26:39). But not long after these words, the temptation hit Him again and again to revert. Each temptation was defeated by the same words, *"Thy will be done"* (Matthew 26:42). Jesus did not allow His feelings to override His faith to do the will of God He knew He was sent on this earth to fulfill. Like Jesus, we must push away our apprehensions and make a total commitment to do whatsoever He tells us. Our focus, Beloved, must be to trust and obey.

Jesus teaches us that we surrender our will to God through prayer. Therefore, as we spend time in prayer, we surrender our will to the Lord and pray like Solomon who declared, *"Trust in the Lord with all thine heart; and lean not unto thine own understanding. In all thy ways acknowledge Him, and He shall direct they paths"* (Proverbs 3:5-6). He gives us an awesome promise here, but the only way for us to see this promise come to fruition is through our obedience unto the Lord.

The word "trust" here means "to lie helpless, facedown." This paints the picture of a servant who is waiting for the master's command in readiness to obey. Herein lies the problem: when we lean on our understanding, we miss His will every time. Solomon is not telling us to turn off our brains and shun our common sense. He is alluding to the fact that we must be careful not to lean on our intellect and what we think by way of past experiences from others we know. After we have prayed, we should always keep that "Nevertheless mindset." *"Not my will, but thy will be done"* (Matthew 26:39).

Our greatest achievement and fulfillment are found in willingly obeying God's will. What do we do when we do not feel like obeying? We allow Him to help us obey Him and His will. He will never leave us by ourselves to do His will simply because He desires to come alongside us/inside us to help us do what He has called us to do. It is okay to ask God to help you want to do His will.

My spiritual father who is now in glory always said, "The safest place in the whole wide world is in the will of God." Beloved, when we take on this mindset, then and only then are we ready to turn our third and final key called "W for Will" over to the Lord!!!

I'm sharing a poem I came across as a means of closing this chapter. Allow this to be a prayer for all of you in Jesus' Name!!

Thy Way, Not Mine
Horatius Bonar

Thy way, not mine, O Lord,
   however dark it be!
Lead me by Thine own Hand,
   choose out the path for me.

Smooth let it be or rough,
   It will be still the best;
Winding or straight, it leads
   Right onward to Thy rest.

I dare not choose my lot;
   I would not, if I might;
Choose Thou for me, my God;
   So shall I walk aright.

The Kingdom that I seek
   Is Thine; so let the way
that leads to it be Thine;
   else I must surely stray.

Take Thou my cup, and it
   with joy or sorrow fill,
as best to Thee may seem;
   Choose Thou my good and ill.

Choose Thou for me my friends,
   my sickness or my health;
Choose Thou my cares for me,

my poverty or wealth.

Not mine, not mine the choice,
In things or great or small;
Be Thou my guide, my strength,
my wisdom, and my all!

Conclusion

People of God, what God desires from you and me is a new man/woman, rather than a new system. He desires yielded individuals, rather than saved individuals. To be sure, it is possible to be saved but not yielded. The charge/cry of Apostle Paul in Romans 12:1-2 is to point out the goal and/or aim of our salvation, which is that you and I may become genuinely yielded to the plan/will of God.

Beloved, I will leave you with this story by Paul Lee Tan. "Back when I was a little boy, we worshipped in a church in East Houston that had a big white sign with broad black letters that read, 'Let go and let God.' I remember sitting there as a child and as a young adolescent looking at those words. In fact, I looked at them every Sunday for several years, 'Let go and let God.' They sounded really great, and I'm sure whoever put them up there wanted them to speak to everybody there. It's a little dubious whether this is the origin, but it seems to be rather well documented: A college student back in the nineteenth century took six postcards and wrote a large letter on each one of the postcards: L - E - T - G - O - D. He then put them on the mantelpiece in his room where he was living at school. One evening a draft blew through the window and the "D" blew away. As he picked it up, what he saw seemed to be a message from God, the secret of the Christian life. Only by letting go can you let God carry out His will in your life."

Beloved, let go, and "Let God drive your BMW!"

Bibliography

Key Word Study. (1991). Chattanooga, TN: AMG Publishers.

Louw, J. P. & Nida, E. A. (1996). *Greek - English Lexicon of the New Testament: Based on Semantic Domains 2nd Edition. Vol 1*. New York: United Bible Societies, 674, Logos Bible Software.

Packer, J. I. (2009). Rediscovering Holiness: Know the fullness of Life with God. Grand Rapid: Baker Books, 69, Kindle Edition.

Renner, Rick (2003). Sparkling Gems from the Greek. Harrison House Publishers.

Sproul. R. C. (1994). The Gospel of God: An Exposition of Romans. Great Britain: Christian Focus Publications, 195, Logos Bible Software.

Stott, John R. W. (2001). The Message of Romans: God's Good News for the World. Downers Grove, IL: InterVarsity Press. 321, Logos Bible Software.

Strong, James. (2010). The New Strong's Exhaustive Concordance of the Bible. Thomas Nelson Publishing.

Swindoll, Charles R. (1998). Ultimate Book of Illustrations & Quotes. Thomas Nelson Publishers, Nashville.

Wilbourne, Rankin. (2016). Union with Christ: The Way to

know and enjoy God. Colorado Springs: David C. Cook, 172.

Verbrugge, Verlyn D. (2000). New International Dictionary of New Testament Theology by Publisher: Zondervan.

Vincent. Marvin R. (1961). Vincent's Word Studies of the New Testament, Vol 3 (Hendrickson Publishers).

About the Author

Dr. Verrick Norwood was born and raised on the South Side of Chicago, IL. Looking back over his life, Dr. Norwood could see God was ordering his steps. After high school, he went to college at Southern IL, University at Edwardsville where he received a BS in Sociology and met Mecheco who later became his wife of now 22 years. They are the parents of two children, Verricka and Joshua. Verricka went home to be with the Lord on December 15, 2017, after being involved in a tragic head-on accident. After moving to California, Dr. Norwood thought he was done with school. However, the Lord had different plans for him.

After giving his life to Christ in 2001, the Lord led him to attend Azusa Pacific University in 2002. In 2006, Dr. Norwood graduated from Azusa Pacific University with a Master of Divinity and later received his Doctor of Ministry in 2012. His dissertation was converted into a book titled *Perfecting the Body: The Role of the Fivefold Ministry Gifts in the Church Today.* It is Dr. Norwood's strong desire to help others experience God's unconditional love, cultivate their spiritual formation, confirm their calling, and discover their spiritual gifts.